About Climate Change

In this workbook, we're about to set off on an exciting journey through the language and ideas that illustrate how climate change impacts our planet! Are you prepared to dive into the excitement? Let's begin our adventure!

The past decade has been the warmest in history. Climate change is increasing global temperatures, but we can help by saving energy and caring for nature.
DID YOU KNOW?
WARNING

<u>ACTIVITY 1</u>

<u>CLIMATE CHANGE:THE BASIC</u>

==Climate change== is like the planet's drama king, stealing the spotlight and demanding our attention!

One of the biggest culprits? The ==Greenhouse Effect== Picture this:pesky gases like carbon dioxide cozying up to our Earth's atmosphere, trapping heat like a blanket on a chilly night, and boom- ==global warming== takes center stage! Our human antics, like burning ==fossil fuels== -coal, oil, and natural gas-are pouring tons of carbon dioxide into the air, cranking up the heat and sending that greenhouse effect into overdrive. Yikes!

DID YOU KNOW?
The greenhouse effect keeps Earth warm, but excess gases from human activities are making it too hot.
Greenhouse Effect

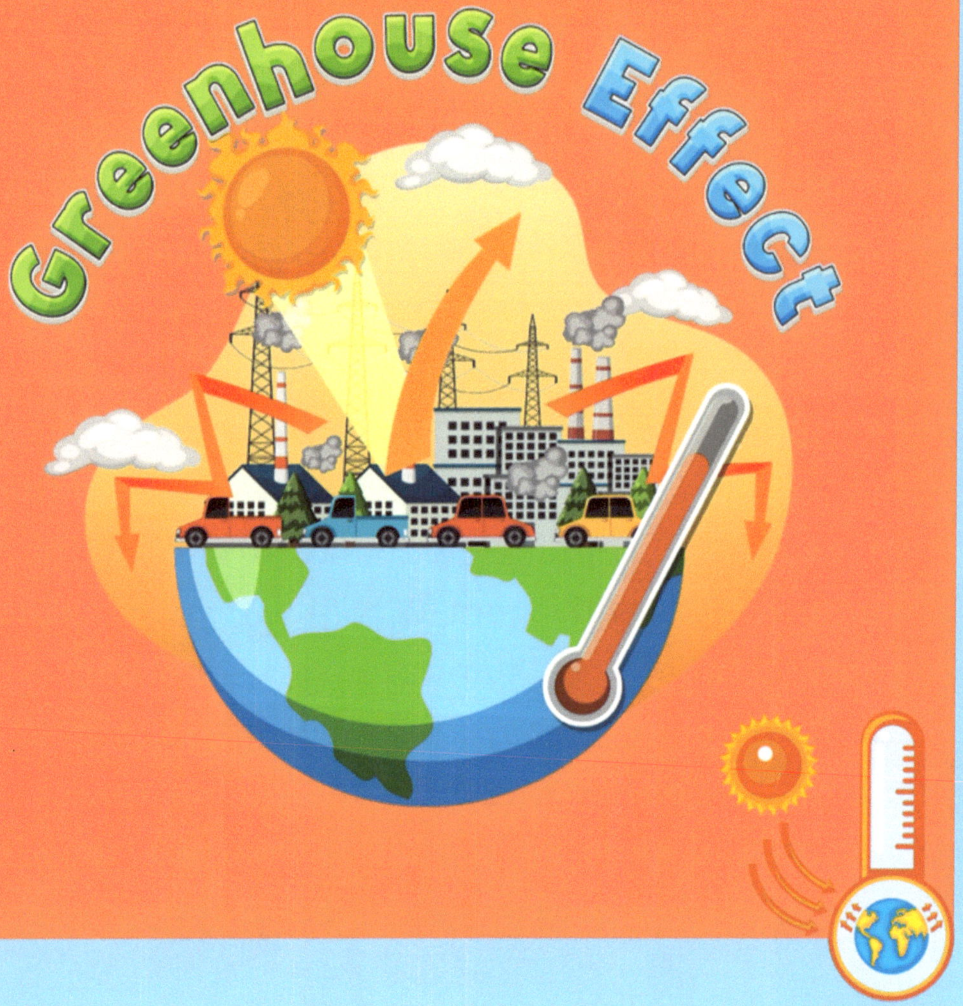

THE GOLDEN TICKET

Climate Change — The planet's sizzling makeover thanks to the greenhouse effect.

Greenhouse Effect — A sizzling hot environmental pickle that's stirring up some wild weather chaos.

Global Warming — The big culprit behind climate change, where sneaky gases turn our atmosphere into a cozy heat trap.

Fossil Fuels — The energy sources that just won't go green.

ACTIVITY 2: BLANKS BE GONE

Dive into the world of nature and find those sneaky missing words! Grab your word bank and let the fill-in-the-blank fun begin!

WORD PARTY!

emissions	climate	greenhouse
fossil	renewable	non-renewable

1. Solar and wind power are examples of__________energy sources that help reduce carbon emissions.

2. Deforestation contributes to the rise of__________gases in the atmosphere, intensifying climate change.

CHECK YOUR ANSWER ON THE "MAGIC DECODER" PAGE (page 9)

emissions	climate	pollutants
methane	renewable	biodiversity

3. Livestock farming produces large amounts of ______________gas, which is even more potent than carbon dioxide.

4. Emissions from_________can harm the environment and human health, contributing to climate change.

5. Protecting natural ecosystems helps preserve our planet's_________.

6. Human activities have significantly altered the Earth's__________, leading to environmental issues.

CHECK YOUR ANSWER ON THE "MAGIC DECODER" PAGE (page 9)

What is CO₂ Pollution?

CO_2 (carbon dioxide) is a gas in the air. It helps keep Earth warm, but too much CO_2 from cars, factories, and burning fuels makes the planet hotter. This is called CO_2 pollution, and it leads to climate change.

Earth Day happens every April 22! People plant trees, clean up trash, and find ways to help our planet. What can YOU do? 🌍🌱

Get ready to flex those brain muscles!. Dive into the paragraph below, pick out four eco-friendly words, and showcase your creativity on the next page. Define them in your quirky way and whip up some images to bring those concepts to life.

Start by shrinking that carbon footprint of yours! Opt for the superhero trio of renewable energy:no greenhouse gases invited!

Let's not forget our leafy friends;keeping those forests intact is key to gobbling up carbon dioxide and saying no to deforestation drama.

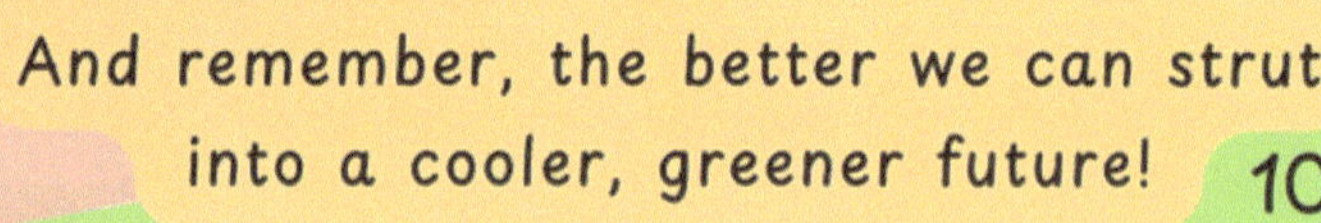

And remember, the better we can strut into a cooler, greener future!

ACTIVITY 3-SHOW AND TELL

The Amazon Rainforest is often called "Earth's lungs" because it helps produce oxygen and absorb carbon dioxide.

WORD

MEANING

IMAGE

DID YOU KNOW?

<u>Less than 3% of all water on Earth is fresh!</u> Most of it is frozen in glaciers, and the rest is salty. That's why saving water is so important.

SHOW AND TELL EXTRAVAGANZA!

Example Response

WORD	MEANING	IMAGE
CARBON FOOTPRINT	This shows how much you affect climate change through your activities	 
HYDROELECTRIC	Using the power of water to make electricity	

More and more countries are choosing solar and wind energy! These clean power sources help reduce pollution and keep the planet healthy.

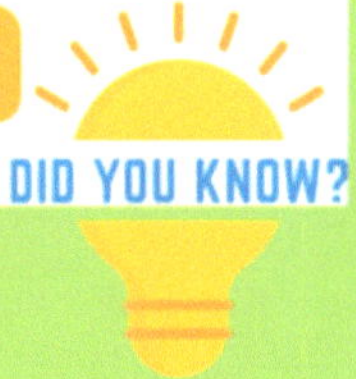

DID YOU KNOW?

Example Response

WORD	MEANING	IMAGE

DEFORESTATION	Cutting down a large number of trees, leading to a loss of forests	
MITIGATE	Taking action to reduce the harmful effects of something	

🐢 <u>Plastic waste can take centuries to break down!</u> That's why recycling and using reusable products helps protect the environment. ♻

MELTING ICE
RISING SEAS!

The Earth is getting hotter, and that makes ice melt. Glaciers and ice caps are turning into water, making the ocean rise. When the sea gets too high, it can flood cities and beaches. But we can help! We can slow it down by using clean energy and taking care of our planet.

ACTIVITY

Fill in the blank: When ice melts, the _______ rises.

Find the answer on page 23

WOW!

✅ Solar power - energy from the sun ☀

✅ Wind power - energy from the wind

✅ Hydropower - energy from moving water 🌊

✅ Geothermal energy - heat from inside the Earth 🌍

✅ Biomass energy - energy from plants and organic waste 🌱

MELTING ICE
NOWHERE TO GO!

Polar bears need ice to live. But the ice is melting, and they are running out of space! When the ice disappears, it gets more challenging for them to find food and rest. They have to swim longer and travel far to survive. But we can help! Using clean energy and protecting nature can slow ice loss and keep their homes safe.

ACTIVITY

1. Fill in the blank: Polar bears need _______ to survive.

2. When ice melts, polar bears have to _______ more to find food.

Find the answer on page 23

WHAT IS HURTING OUR PLANET ?

OUR PLANET IS BEAUTIFUL, BUT SOME THINGS MAKE IT SICK. HERE ARE A FEW BIG PROBLEMS THAT HURT THE EARTH:

Dirty Air - Cars, factories, and burning fuels fill the air with smoke and chemicals. These pollutants make it harder to breathe and contribute to global warming..

Too Much Trash - People throw away too much plastic and waste. Some of it is in the ocean, hurting animals and polluting the water.

Cutting Down Too Many Trees
Trees clean the air and give us oxygen, but people are cutting down forests too fast. This leaves animals without homes and makes climate change worse.

Oceans in Danger - Overfishing and pollution harm sea creatures. Coral reefs are fading, and many fish species are decreasing in number.

Wasting Water - Clean water is precious, but people waste it by leaving taps on, overusing it, or polluting rivers and lakes.

WHAT CAN WE DO? 🌱

SMALL CHANGES HELP A LOT! RECYCLE, WALK INSTEAD OF DRIVE, PLANT TREES, AND SAVE WATER. IF WE ALL HELP, WE CAN PROTECT OUR PLANET FOR THE FUTURE!

GOOD
FOR THE PLANET

RIDING A BIKE

PLANTING TREES

SOLAR PANELS

RECYCLING

BAD
FOR THE PLANET

USING TOO MUCH PLASTIC

CUTTING DOWN TREES

LEAVING THE LIGHTS
ON WHEN NOT
NEEDED

THROWING TRASH IN
NATURE

Mission: Save the Planet!

Every hero has a mission! **Draw yourself** as a Planet Hero completing an important mission—planting trees, cleaning up trash, or saving animals!

Question 1:
What helps reduce pollution?
A) Throwing trash in the ocean 🌊
B) Planting more trees 🌳
C) Using more plastic bottles 🥤

Question 2:
Which energy source is the cleanest?
A) Coal ⛏
B) Solar power ☀
C) Gasoline ⛽

Question 3:
What happens when we cut down too many trees?
A) The air gets cleaner 🍃
B) Animals lose their homes 🦊
C) More ice appears in the Arctic ❄

Question 4:
How can you help the planet every day?
A) Turn off the lights when you don't need them 💡
B) Let the water run while brushing your teeth 🚰
C) Use plastic bags instead of reusable ones 🛍

✏ Bonus Question:
Name one small action YOU can do to help the Earth!

How to Be
a Planet-Saving Superhero?

REMEMBER

You hold the superhero cape to create a positive splash in our environment, and guess what? The first step on this epic mission is stacking up your knowledge like a pro!

Recycle Like a Pro. Sort your trash correctly. The planet will thank you for helping to keep it clean and green.

Thank You for Reading! 🌍 💚

If you enjoyed this book, we would truly appreciate your review on Amazon. Your feedback helps us create more fun and educational books for young Planet Heroes like you!

Remember, every small action counts. Together, we can create a brighter, greener future! 🌱✨

Ditch the plastic! Say no to single-use stuff. Reusable bottles and bags - saving the planet in style!

Unplug and Chill Turn off lights and gadgets when you're not using them. Less energy consumption means fewer climate-related issues.

Are you ready to step up and be a planet-saver?

Quiz Answers

1. B) Planting more trees 🌳
2. B) Solar power ☀️
3. B) Animals lose their homes 🦊
4. A) Turn off the lights 💡

Check Your Answers

- Page 15: Ocean
- Page 16: Ice, Swim

If you want to use this book for educational purposes, please contact Treedopress@gmail.com

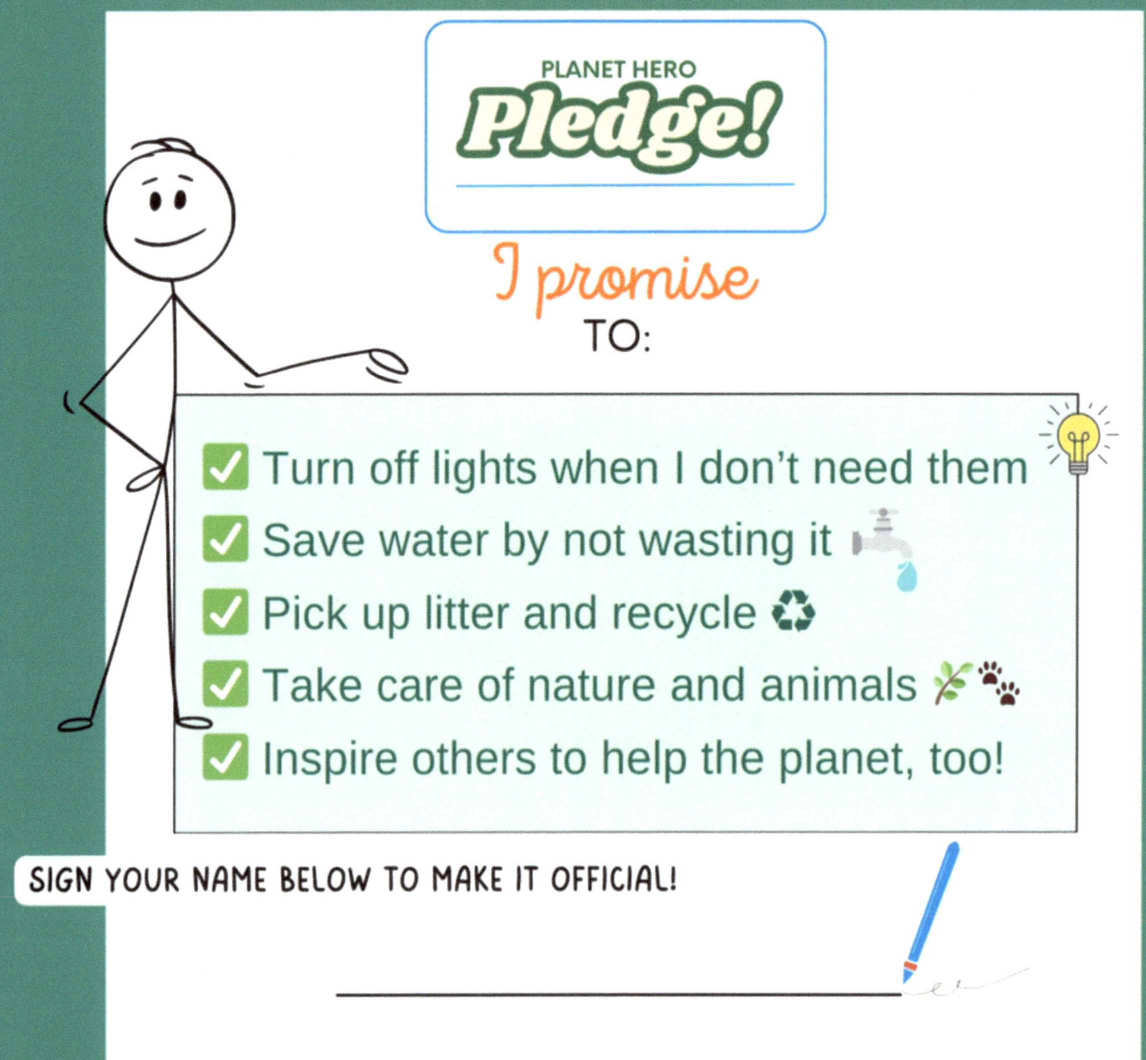
PLANET HERO
Pledge!
I promise
TO:
Turn off lights when I don't need them
Save water by not wasting it
Pick up litter and recycle
Take care of nature and animals
Inspire others to help the planet, too!
SIGN YOUR NAME BELOW TO MAKE IT OFFICIAL!

CONGRATULATIONS
PLANET HERO

You have learned so much about climate change and how to help protect our planet. Now it is time to celebrate your achievement
💚 Write your name on the certificate
💚 Share your knowledge with friends and family
💚 Keep making eco-friendly choices every day
Every small action counts. Together, we can make a difference! 🌱

Planet Hero Certificate

Awarded to: _______________________________ ✏️

For Learning About

Climate Change & Helping the Earth 💚

Thank you for being a Planet Hero and making a difference! Every small action counts— together, we can protect our planet! 🌱✨

Date: _______________ 

9 798301 757617